GW01402829

Original title:
A New Beginning

Copyright © 2024 Swan Charm
All rights reserved.

Author: Kaido Väinamäe
ISBN HARDBACK: 978-9916-89-778-2
ISBN PAPERBACK: 978-9916-89-779-9
ISBN EBOOK: 978-9916-89-780-5

Blessings in the Waters of Change

In the flow of rivers wide,
We seek truth, our hearts abide.
Every wave, a whispered prayer,
Guided by the love laid bare.

Through the storm and through the strife,
Waves remind us of new life.
In each drop, a sacred spark,
Leading us out of the dark.

Oceans vast, a boundless grace,
Each ripple bears a warm embrace.
Trust the tides that come and go,
In their depths, the light shall glow.

From the shores, we rise anew,
Casting fears, faith's path is true.
In the currents, blessings flow,
Nurtured seeds of hope shall grow.

When we wander, lost at sea,
Let the waters set us free.
In the depths where spirits soar,
Blessings wait on every shore.

Covenant of the Heart

In the silence, whispers flow,
A promise made, a seed to sow.
Hearts entwined, bound by grace,
In love's embrace, we find our place.

Through trials faced, we stand as one,
In faith we rise, our journey begun.
With every prayer, our spirits soar,
A testament of love, forevermore.

Everlasting Light

In shadows deep, the light will shine,
A guiding flame, a spark divine.
Through darkest nights, hope shall rise,
Illuminating all our skies.

Every soul seeks that gentle glow,
A beacon bright, where mercy flows.
With open hearts, we share this grace,
Everlasting light, our sacred space.

The Prayer of the Rising Sun

As dawn awakes, a prayer we raise,
In gentle light, we sing His praise.
With every breath, we seek the day,
In joyful hope, we find our way.

The sun ascends, a promise new,
In warmth and love, His mercies true.
With gratitude, we walk this path,
The rising sun, our joyous hearth.

Into the Embrace of Tomorrow

With open arms, we greet the day,
In every step, He guides our way.
The future calls, with whispered dreams,
In faith we trust, or so it seems.

Through trials faced, we learn to grow,
With hearts aligned, His grace we show.
Into tomorrow, hand in hand,
Together strong, we make our stand.

Emblems of Transformation

In the garden of our soul, we grow,
Seeds of faith in the heart's soft glow.
Each trial a chisel, shaping the clay,
Transforming shadow into the day.

With whispered prayers and gentle grace,
We rise anew, in love's embrace.
Wounds like petals, unfold in time,
Bearing witness to the divine.

From ashes, we find the will to stand,
Rebirth through trials, guided by hand.
In the storm's eye, we hear the call,
To break the chains and rise above all.

Mirrors of truth reflect the light,
In the journey from wrong to right.
Each step a dance, a sacred rite,
Emblems of change, shining bright.

So trust the path, the winding road,
For through the struggle, we share the load.
In unity, we shall transform,
Together, we weather, we are reborn.

Spiritual Renaissance

Awake within the silent sea,
New dawn breaking, we are free.
The spirit stirs, in whispers low,
In every heart, a sacred glow.

With open hearts, we seek the light,
Transcending darkness, embracing sight.
In prayers lifted, our souls unite,
A renaissance born of pure delight.

The echoes of the ancient wise,
Guide us gently toward the skies.
With every breath, divinity sings,
Awakening hope, on faith's bright wings.

In the tapestry of night and day,
We find our truth along the way.
Resilient souls in quest sublime,
Awaking dreams that withstand time.

Thus, let us journey hand in hand,
Through valleys deep, across the land.
In every heartbeat, a tale reborn,
Together, we rise with each new morn.

From Darkness to Light

In shadows deep, where sorrows dwell,
There lies a truth we know so well.
Through pain and loss, the soul will rise,
Transforming tears to hopeful skies.

The dawn awakens, softly near,
A whispered promise, calm and clear.
From depths where silence once confined,
We find the strength to leave behind.

In brokenness, we seek the grace,
Emerging whole in love's embrace.
For every night must yield to day,
As light dispels the dark away.

With courage bold, we face our fears,
In the journey, wiped are tears.
Through every trial, a path unfolds,
A story of light, in faith retold.

So lift your eyes, the dawn is here,
Embrace the light without a fear.
From darkness deep, our spirits soar,
In love awakened, forevermore.

The Blessed Beginning

In every dawn, a gift appears,
Wrapped in hope, dispelling fears.
The world reborn, a canvas bright,
Unfolds before our yearning sight.

With every breath, a sacred song,
A melody where we belong.
In gratitude, our spirits rise,
Embracing joy beneath the skies.

The gentle touch of heaven's hand,
Guides us forward, heart to stand.
With open arms, we greet the day,
In every moment, find our way.

In kindness shared, love's gentle spark,
Illuminates each shadowed dark.
Let's walk together, hand in hand,
In this blessed life, let us stand.

A journey vast, with purpose clear,
In every heartbeat, we draw near.
The blessed beginning, never end,
In unity, our spirits mend.

Whispers of the Divine

In silence I hear, the softest call,
A gentle guidance, through the rise and fall.
In prayerful moments, the spirit speaks,
With every whisper, the heart it seeks.

The stars bear witness, to paths unknown,
In sacred stillness, our truth is shown.
Echoes of mercy, in the night's embrace,
Each breath a blessing, touched by grace.

Through trials faced, the light will shine,
In love's embrace, our souls entwine.
With faith as our anchor, we rise and soar,
In the whispers of the Divine, we explore.

The Covenant of Change

In seasons turning, the promise stands,
A sacred covenant, held in loving hands.
With every sunset, hope is reborn,
In the dance of time, we're never forlorn.

The winds of change, they whisper low,
Carrying dreams, where rivers flow.
In every ending, a chance to grow,
As hearts awaken, to let love show.

With every heartbeat, the story unfolds,
In the tapestry woven, the truth it holds.
Embrace the shift, let go of the past,
In the covenant of change, love will last.

Lighthouses of the Soul

In the darkest night, they stand so bright,
Guiding the weary, with their pure light.
Each flicker of hope, a beacon strong,
Lighthouses of the soul, where we belong.

Through stormy seas, and tempests wild,
They whisper comfort, like a mother's child.
With wisdom vast, they effortlessly share,
In the calm of their glow, we're held with care.

For every journey, there lies a sign,
A reminder of love, so pure, divine.
Let's follow the light, and never stray far,
In the lighthouses of the soul, we are.

The Sacred Cycle

Life flows like rivers, in a sacred dance,
A circle of wonder, a blessed chance.
From dawn till dusk, the cycle spins,
In every ending, a new life begins.

The moonlight whispers, of time's embrace,
In shadows and light, we seek our place.
With each turn of seasons, we learn to see,
The sacred cycle, of you and me.

In birth and rebirth, our spirits rise,
Through trials faced, we reach for the skies.
Embracing change, with open hearts,
In the sacred cycle, love never departs.

From Darkness to Light

In shadows deep where whispers dwell,
A prayer arises, a sacred spell.
The dawn breaks forth, a gentle grace,
Illuminating every space.

From trials fierce, our spirits soar,
Through faith we find the open door.
With every step, the path grows bright,
We walk together, hand in light.

Though tempests rage and storms may cry,
We lift our hearts, and fears comply.
For in His arms, we find our rest,
In darkest nights, we are truly blessed.

Miracles of the Morning

The sun ascends with golden rays,
Awakening life in wondrous ways.
Each flower blooms, a hymn of praise,
To greet the dawn, our hearts ablaze.

The dew-kissed grass, a sacred sign,
Reflects the love, divine design.
Each breath we take, a sacred gift,
In morning light, our spirits lift.

With every chirp, the world sings bright,
In tune with grace, our souls take flight.
These miracles, though small they seem,
In every heart, ignite the dream.

The Holy Voyage

Embarking on this sacred quest,
With faith as compass, we are blessed.
Through waves of doubt, we navigate,
Towards shores of love, we elevate.

The stars above, a guiding light,
In darkest seas, they shine so bright.
Together in this blessed crew,
We seek the truth, our hearts anew.

With every gust, a breath of grace,
We find His presence in this space.
Though storms may rage and fears may rise,
We'll trust His plan, and reach the skies.

Signs of the Infinite

In every leaf that dances free,
A whisper speaks of mystery.
The mountains high, the valleys low,
In nature's arms, His love does flow.

The stars above in vast expanse,
Invite our hearts to dream and dance.
Each fleeting moment, a holy spark,
Illuminating shadows dark.

In kindness shared and hands that heal,
We find the truth, we learn to feel.
The signs abound, in heart's embrace,
Infinite love in every space.

Light After the Storm

In the darkest hours, a whisper calls,
Hope arises as the thunder falls.
Through the pain, a beacon shines,
Guiding souls where love entwines.

Raindrops weep upon the ground,
Yet in each tear, grace is found.
The skies clear, revealing grace,
In the heart, light finds its place.

After the tempest, the dawn breaks free,
In the stillness, we come to see.
Redemption blooms in the wake of strife,
A testament to the gift of life.

Blossoms of the Eternal

In sacred gardens, the blossoms grow,
Rooted in love, they softly glow.
Each petal whispers, a prayer divine,
In the stillness, we find the sign.

From the soil of faith, new life is born,
In every heart, His light adorns.
Through seasons changing, the blooms extend,
Eternal spring, where souls transcend.

In the silence, the truth unfurls,
Mirror of the heavens, in this world.
Embracing all, our spirits soar,
Blossoms of the eternal, forevermore.

Embracing the Unknown

In shadows deep, there lies the grace,
A journey unfolds, in time and space.
With faith as our map, we venture forth,
To find new light, to know our worth.

The path may twist, the road may bend,
Yet within uncertainty, hearts will mend.
With every step, a lesson learned,
In the fire of courage, our spirits turned.

Embrace the mysteries, let go of fear,
In the silence, His voice is near.
Trust in the love that leads us on,
For in the unknown, we have begun.

Testament of the Heart

In the quiet whispers, truth reveals,
A testament written, the spirit heals.
With words of kindness, and hands that share,
Love becomes the answer to every prayer.

As seasons change, and time flows on,
The heart remembers, the love stays strong.
Each moment treasured, a sacred mark,
Within the light, we spark the dark.

From trials faced, to joys bestowed,
In every heartbeat, His love we sow.
Our lives, a canvas, painted bright,
A testament of grace, our endless light.

The Fountain of New Life

In the garden where waters flow,
Life springs forth in gentle glow.
Each drop whispers tales of grace,
Renewing hearts in tender space.

The roots entwine, a sacred trust,
From deadened soil, we rise from dust.
Awash in blessings, we stand tall,
Embracing love that binds us all.

The fountain flows with hope divine,
Its waters cleanse through love's design.
Each sip a promise, pure and bright,
Guiding souls from dark to light.

In the stillness, prayers ascend,
Finding solace, heart to mend.
While life may falter, spirits soar,
In the fountain, we are restored.

As dawn breaks forth, so do we rise,
Reflecting grace beneath the skies.
The fountain sings a sacred song,
In unity, we all belong.

Beneath the Canopy of Stars

Underneath a vast expanse,
Whispers of heaven in our glance.
Stars align, their light a guide,
In the dark, our hopes abide.

Each twinkle tells of dreams untold,
Of faith, of love, of hearts so bold.
The cosmos breathes a gentle sigh,
Warming souls as night drifts by.

In the stillness, prayers take flight,
Carried forth into the night.
Beneath this cosmic tapestry,
We find our place in history.

As constellations weave their tales,
We walk together, hearts as sails.
Guided by the light above,
Awash in the warmth of endless love.

In silence, trust becomes our spark,
Illuminating paths through dark.
Beneath the stars, a promise stays,
Hope eternal in endless praise.

The Spirit's Awakening

In the quiet of the morn,
A whisper stirs, a soul reborn.
The spirit breathes in fresh delight,
Igniting hearts with sacred light.

Like dawn's first rays that chase the night,
Awakening shadows, bringing bright.
With each new breath, we find our way,
Embracing love in every day.

The essence flows, like rivers stream,
Filling hearts with hope's pure dream.
In every moment, grace unfolds,
Healing wounds that time upholds.

With open hearts, we rise as one,
In unity, our battles won.
The spirit whispers through the trees,
Bringing solace on gentle breeze.

In the journey, we learn to see,
The beauty in each mystery.
The spirit's song forever stays,
Guiding us through all our days.

Promises of the Dawn

As night surrenders to the light,
Whispers of dawn chase away fright.
Promises woven in dawn's embrace,
Bring forth hope, our hearts' true grace.

Golden rays break through the shell,
In each heartbeat, we find the swell.
The morning's glow a tender kiss,
A reminder of eternal bliss.

With every step, the world awakes,
A canvas new that love remakes.
In the silence, joy will reign,
Through every joy, through every pain.

The dawn unveils a chance to mend,
In every heart, a sacred blend.
As shadows fade, we find our way,
In the warmth of each new day.

In promises made beneath the sun,
Together we rise, forever one.
With open hearts and hands outspread,
Embracing the light that lies ahead.

Echoes of Grace

In the quiet whisper of the night,
Faith illuminates the soul's delight.
Hearts entwined in sacred embrace,
We find our strength in echoes of grace.

The dawn unfolds a promise true,
With every breath, we start anew.
Guided by love, we seek the light,
In every shadow, hope takes flight.

Moments of peace, like softest rain,
Wash away the lingering pain.
Together we rise, with spirits aligned,
In the arms of mercy, joy we find.

Through trials fierce, we stand as one,
Beneath the watchful eye of the sun.
With gratitude, our voices blend,
In harmony, our prayers ascend.

Eternal bonds, in His name we weave,
In the heart's tapestry, we believe.
With every echo, His love we trace,
Forever blessed by echoes of grace.

The Divine Tapestry

Threads of life, in colors bright,
Woven together, a sacred light.
Each story shared, a strand of care,
In the divine tapestry, love we declare.

Moments of joy, and whispers of pain,
In the loom of faith, we find our gain.
Every heartbeat, a stitch of grace,
Unity emerges in this holy space.

Hands reaching out across the divide,
In love's embrace, we shall abide.
With every challenge, we understand,
The beauty of life in God's gentle hand.

Mountains may rise, rivers may bend,
In His presence, all hearts mend.
Walking together, our spirits set free,
In the divine tapestry, you and me.

As we gather, hope starts to bloom,
In the promise of faith, we find our room.
Each thread a blessing, a wondrous place,
Woven forever in the divine grace.

Renewal in the Stillness

In the quiet moments, we seek His face,
Where silence breathes, our spirits trace.
The world fades away, time stands still,
In renewal's embrace, we find His will.

Gentle whispers in the evening air,
In every pause, He teaches care.
Nature's symphony, a sacred song,
In stillness, we realize where we belong.

Broken hearts mend in twilight's glow,
As grace pours in, like a river's flow.
Restoration blooms, with love we fill,
In the depths of silence, hope is our thrill.

A journey inward, where truth resides,
In prayerful stillness, our spirit abides.
The light of faith guides us true,
In renewal's grace, we are born anew.

With each breath drawn, we feel the peace,
In the stillness, our worries cease.
Embracing the moment, we're wrapped in love,
A sacred renewal, blessed from above.

Blessed Returns

The wandering spirit seeks the home,
In every step, where grace may roam.
Returning to the fold, we find our place,
In the warmth of love, blessed returns embrace.

Paths may twist, and seasons change,
Yet in His heart, we rearrange.
With open arms, He waits for all,
In the dance of life, we hear the call.

Stories woven, across the miles,
In gatherings blessed, with joyful smiles.
Hearts uplifted in shared refrain,
In togetherness, we rise again.

Through valleys deep, and mountains high,
Faith leads us through, as days pass by.
With every return, a tale unfolds,
In love's embrace, a destiny bold.

The journey matters, each step we take,
In the circle of life, the bonds we make.
With gratitude, we lift our voice,
In blessed returns, we rejoice.

Ascending from Doubt

In shadows deep, my heart did yearn,
For whispers soft, for truths to learn.
I reached for light, through faith I sought,
To rise above the endless thought.

The burdened soul, it longs to soar,
To break the chains, to seek much more.
On wings of trust, I climbed the skies,
To find the peace where spirit lies.

I cast aside my fears of night,
Embracing love, embracing light.
With every step, I left behind,
The doubts that plagued my troubled mind.

In stillness found, the voice within,
A gentle call, a new begin.
With open heart, I take the flight,
Ascending high, into the light.

Awakening the Dawn

As dawn awakes, the world shall glow,
With whispered grace, the heavens flow.
Each ray of sun, a gift in hand,
A promise made, a gentle stand.

The morn ignites the silent earth,
In praise we rise, in joyful mirth.
The night retreats, its shadows flee,
In sacred warmth, our souls are free.

From darkness sprung, the light returns,
In every heart, a fire that burns.
Awoken dreams, like flowers bloom,
In every heart, dispelling gloom.

With open eyes, we see the grace,
In every moment, God's embrace.
Awakening dawn, our spirits sing,
In unity, all praises bring.

The First Light of Creation

In silence deep, the void was still,
A breath divine began to fill.
From nothingness, the cosmos spun,
The first light danced, all had begun.

A tapestry, of stars and skies,
In vibrant hues, the beauty flies.
Each atom sings, a holy sound,
In sacred rhythm, all is found.

With every pulse, life's breath awoke,
A tapestry of wondrous hope.
In joy we bask, in love's embrace,
Creation sings, the birth of grace.

The first light shines, ignites the dark,
In every heart, a holy spark.
As spirits rise, we heed the call,
The light of love, embracing all.

Resurrection of the Spirit

In the silence of a weeping night,
A whisper came, a spark of light.
Through darkest valleys, hope arose,
In tender grace, the spirit grows.

The chains of doubt, they fell away,
In faith reborn, we greet the day.
A guiding hand, a gentle touch,
In every soul, our God's sweet hush.

From ashes lost, the fire ignites,
With every breath, the spirit writes.
A song of joy, a dance sublime,
In love's embrace, we transcend time.

Resurrection flows, the heart renewed,
In endless grace, our spirits food.
With open arms, we greet the dawn,
In unity, our spirits drawn.

The Sacred Unfolding

In silence, the dawn breaks light,
Whispers of grace fill the air,
Each petal unfurls with care,
The heart blooms in holy sight.

In shadows, the spirit takes flight,
Guided by a gentle hand,
Through valleys of faith we stand,
Embracing the love so bright.

The stars above sing of peace,
As prayers rise to heaven's door,
In unity, our hopes soar,
In sacred moments, we cease.

The river flows with clear intent,
Washing away the doubts inside,
With every ripple, we confide,
In the warmth of love's descent.

Together we journey on this path,
Hand in hand, we've come so far,
In the midst of the weary spar,
We find strength in each other's wrath.

Celestial Horizons

Beneath the vast, eternal skies,
We seek the light of sacred lore,
With faith that opens every door,
Our hearts sing out, it never dies.

Upon the hills where angels tread,
Whispers of wisdom fill the night,
A tapestry of purest light,
In every soul, a story led.

Through trials, the spirit is forged,
Like gold refined in fire's embrace,
In the depths of love's warm grace,
Our doubts and fears are all purged.

The universe in harmony,
Each star a promise of the Divine,
Our lives entwined, a sacred line,
In every breath, a symphony.

From depths of night to dawn's new glow,
We rise with hope, our hearts unite,
In this dance of sacred light,
Together in faith, we will grow.

The First Breath of Faith

In the stillness, the heart begins,
A whisper stirs, a sacred call,
With every rise, with every fall,
The journey starts where light ne'er sins.

The first breath held with hopeful grace,
A flicker of trust in every soul,
In seeking truth, we become whole,
In every heart, a holy place.

Mountains tremble, the earth stands still,
In moments of doubt, love shines bright,
Guiding us through shadows of night,
In faith, we find our steadfast will.

With open hands, we seek the light,
In unity, our spirits blend,
Embracing all who choose to mend,
Together we'll walk through the fight.

Each dawn unfolds a brand new chance,
To dance upon the sacred ground,
In every heartbeat, love is found,
In the rhythm of faith's sweet trance.

Rise from the Ruins

From ashes cold, a spark ignites,
In darkness, we find the light,
With every struggle, a new sight,
Our spirits soar to greater heights.

Through broken dreams and shattered stone,
A war of faith begins to rise,
With every tear, we claim the skies,
Together, we are not alone.

The wounds we bear, now healed and whole,
In unity, we forge anew,
From rubble, life begins to bloom,
With love's pure grace, we reach our goal.

In every heart, a flame will burn,
A testament to strength within,
With every loss, we find our kin,
In bitter turns, we now discern.

Through trials faced, we stand in pride,
Embracing hope, we carve our way,
In faith's embrace, we find the day,
From ruins, we will now abide.

Dawn's Gentle Whisper

In silence, dawn unfolds its grace,
A soft embrace of light's warm face.
The world awakens, hearts aligned,
In every breath, Your love we find.

The sun ascends, a golden hue,
A promise made, forever true.
With each new day, our spirits rise,
Reflections of the endless skies.

In dew-kissed fields, Your blessings flow,
The sacred dance of life we know.
Through whispered prayers, our souls ignite,
A journey guided by Your light.

The dawn brings hope, a fresh new start,
United we stand, one beating heart.
In gratitude, our voices soar,
To honor You, forevermore.

Threads of the Infinite

In every moment, woven tight,
The threads of love reveal their light.
Each gentle bond, a sacred tie,
Connecting us with earth and sky.

With faith, we stitch our dreams anew,
Embroidering life with shades of You.
Through trials faced, the fabric's strong,
In unity, we find our song.

The tapestry, a sacred lore,
Of countless lives, forevermore.
Each thread a story, soft and bright,
Illuminated by Your light.

As time unfolds, the fabric sways,
In love we trust, through all our days.
The threads unite, our hearts entwined,
In the infinite, our souls aligned.

Ascending in Faith

With every step, we climb the height,
Embracing faith, our guiding light.
Through valleys deep and mountains wide,
In You, O Lord, we will abide.

A path illuminated bright,
Through trials faced, we gain our sight.
In trust, we journey, hand in hand,
With faith as firm as shifting sand.

As clouds may gather, storms may roar,
We find our shelter at Your door.
With every prayer that soars above,
We rise in strength, the wings of love.

Our spirits lifted, hearts ablaze,
In every moment, song of praise.
Together strong, we face the day,
Ascending higher in Your way.

The Light Between Us

In shadows cast, Your light remains,
A shining beacon through our pains.
The love we share, a sacred glow,
In each reflection, truth we know.

Through trials faced and tears embraced,
In every moment, grace is traced.
The bonds of hearts that intertwine,
Illuminate, divine design.

As stars above, so bright and clear,
Your whispers call when hope feels near.
In quietude, we find our place,
Together journeying, seeking grace.

The light between us, ever strong,
In harmony, we sing our song.
With faith our anchor, love our trust,
In Your embrace, we rise, we must.

In the Light of New Horizons

In dawn's embrace, we rise anew,
With hearts ignited by love so true.
The heavens whisper, guiding our way,
In every moment, hope holds sway.

Fields of gold stretch far and wide,
In faith we walk, with none to hide.
Together we seek, with eyes refined,
New horizons call, our spirits aligned.

Through valleys dark and skies of grey,
Our trust unwavering, come what may.
With every step, we find our place,
In sacred whispers, we feel His grace.

Promises spoken in softest tones,
Rekindle dreams, awaken our bones.
In the light of dawn, all fears subside,
In unity's strength, our souls abide.

Hearts united, we journey on,
With faith as our guide, we'll greet the dawn.
New horizons beckon, oh, how they gleam,
In the light of hope, we'll build our dream.

Faith's Reawakening

In shadows deep, a spark ignites,
Faith's gentle hand brings forth the lights.
With every whisper from above,
We feel the pulse of sacred love.

Moments fleeting, yet so profound,
In silence wrapped, our souls are found.
Reawakening in stillness pure,
The heart now seeks, the spirit sure.

Through trials faced, our strength will grow,
In faith's embrace, we come to know.
The path is winding, yet we shall tread,
For in His arms, we are led.

With each sunrise, anew we rise,
Awakening dreams, breaking the ties.
In sacred journeys, onward we go,
With faith as our compass, hearts all aglow.

Together we sing, in harmony's song,
In love's great tapestry, we all belong.
A reawakening, a gift divine,
In faith's embrace, our spirits shine.

Threads of Destiny

In weaving light, our fates entwine,
Threads of gold, by design divine.
Every moment, a choice we make,
In the loom of time, our hearts awake.

Destiny whispers through silent night,
Guiding our paths towards the light.
With every heartbeat, a sign unfolds,
In the tapestry of faith, we behold.

Each thread a prayer, in colors bright,
Stitched with hope, in love's pure sight.
In every challenge, a lesson learned,
As we embrace what the heart has yearned.

Through trials faced, we grow in grace,
With faith as our anchor in every place.
Hand in hand, we walk the line,
In threads of destiny, our souls align.

Together we stand, unwavering and strong,
In the fabric of life, we all belong.
With every stitch, we celebrate,
In the threads of destiny, we create.

The Symphony of Renewal

In nature's choir, a song takes flight,
The symphony of renewal, pure delight.
With every note, a heart will heal,
In harmony's dance, our souls reveal.

The rivers flow, a gentle refrain,
With every drop, the earth regains.
In sacred circles, we shall unite,
In love's embrace, we find our light.

Through seasons' change, we rise anew,
Each dawn a promise, bright and true.
With faith as our melody, hope in our hands,
Together we thrive, as love expands.

In whispered winds, the spirits call,
In the symphony of life, we rise and fall.
With every sigh, a prayer ascends,
In the music of renewal, our soul transcends.

Together we sing, the song of the free,
In the symphony of all that can be.
With open hearts, our voices soar,
In the rhythm of life, forevermore.

The Circle of Grace

In the arms of love we dwell,
Bound by faith, a sacred spell.
Hope ignites the darkest night,
In His presence, we find light.

Grace flows down like gentle rain,
Washing us of every pain.
Hearts united, spirits soar,
In this circle, forevermore.

With each prayer, our voices rise,
Echoing through the endless skies.
In His mercy, we discover,
We are sisters, we are brothers.

Through trials faced, our souls are strong,
In His love, we all belong.
Trust the path that leads us home,
In this grace, we are never alone.

So let us walk with humble hearts,
As grace envelops and imparts.
Joined together, hand in hand,
In the circle, we shall stand.

Glimpses of the Eternal

In shadows cast by fleeting time,
We seek the truth, a love divine.
Fragments of light, a sacred touch,
In silence speaks so very much.

Stars that twinkle in the night,
Whisper secrets, pure and bright.
Moments etched in infinity,
Glimpses of what is yet to be.

Through valleys deep and mountains high,
The spirit soars, will never die.
Each heartbeat, a gift profound,
In every breath, His love is found.

In sacred spaces, we are led,
With open hearts, we journey ahead.
The eternal calls, we hear the sound,
In these glimpses, joy is found.

As rivers flow and seasons change,
The eternal truth will rearrange.
In every sorrow, every tear,
We glimpse His love, forever near.

Land of Milk and Honey

In the promise of a land so sweet,
Where burdens lifted, hearts will meet.
Flowing with love and endless grace,
In this haven, we find our place.

Fields that bloom with colors bright,
Underneath the sun's warm light.
Nourished by faith, we grow and thrive,
In this land, we come alive.

Streams of mercy gently flow,
In His blessings, we overflow.
Unity and hope we seek,
In harmony, the strong and meek.

As we wander through the days,
Guided by His holy ways.
In every heart, a song will rise,
In this land, our spirits fly.

Together we shall share the feast,
From greatest to the very least.
In this promise, we stand as one,
In the light of the setting sun.

Shattered Chains

From the depths of despair we rise,
Free from burdens, we find skies.
Chains of doubt, they fall away,
In His love, we greet the day.

Each scar a story, every fight,
Transforms our pain into the light.
Hope rekindled, we embrace,
In the promise of His grace.

Shattered chains, a heart set free,
In His presence, we truly see.
Stronger now, we stand with pride,
In His love, we shall abide.

Let the darkness fade away,
In His glory, we shall stay.
Bound together, hand in hand,
In freedom's song, forever stand.

With every step, a new dawn brings,
Joyful hearts, we rise and sing.
In every trial, courage gained,
In His promise, chains are drained.

Mosaic of Mercy

In grace we find our crafted light,
A tapestry of love in sight.
Each thread of kindness interwove,
A masterpiece of Heaven's love.

When hearts are broken, hope will rise,
Through humble hands, the service ties.
With every act, a spark ignites,
Creating peace in darkest nights.

Forgiveness flows, a gentle stream,
A healing balm, a sacred dream.
In whispered prayers, our voices soar,
To mend the world, forevermore.

In shadows cast, our faith shall stand,
Embraced within the Maker's hand.
Unity, our guiding song,
In mercy's heart, we all belong.

As raindrops fall on thirsty ground,
The seeds of hope are freely found.
Together, we shape divinity,
In every face, humanity.

The Call of the Future

O rising dawn, the light shall break,
Awakening dreams for all our sake.
With every step, we dare to tread,
Into the path where love is spread.

Voices lifted, a choir born,
In unity, a new world sworn.
The vision clear, our spirits wise,
To seek the truth beneath the skies.

Let hands unite, a strength profound,
In every heart, a promise found.
The journey long, with faith our guide,
A beacon bright, where hope abides.

Through trials faced, we rise anew,
With courage fierce, our purpose true.
A world reborn in healing grace,
Together we shall find our place.

Embrace the change, let fears retreat,
In love's embrace, the future sweet.
In every heartbeat, stories blend,
A legacy that will transcend.

Echoes of the Unseen

In whispers soft, the spirit calls,
Through unseen realms where silence falls.
A gentle nudge, a sign bestowed,
Awakening paths that we explore.

The light that flickers, shadows cast,
A truth unveiled, our hearts amassed.
In every moment, presence felt,
In sacred stillness, love is dealt.

Each heartbeat echoes, a sacred sound,
A language pure that knows no bound.
Through trials faced, we rise and learn,
In hidden places, candles burn.

The unseen threads that bind us tight,
In every soul, a spark of light.
In unity, we find our grace,
Together walking, face to face.

A tapestry of hope unfolds,
In every story, love retold.
Through unseen echoes, we shall rise,
In faith's embrace, forever wise.

The Veil of the New

Behind the veil, the dawn awakes,
In luminous hues, the spirit breaks.
A future bright, where shadows fade,
In every heart, new dreams are laid.

The gentle touch of grace descends,
A river's flow that never ends.
In sacred trust, we join as one,
Beneath the watchful, caring sun.

With open arms, we welcome change,
In every moment, paths arrange.
The veil lifts high, revealing truth,
In every age, the wisdom of youth.

As seasons shift, we learn and grow,
In faith's embrace, our spirits glow.
The new horizon calls us near,
With courage strong, dispelling fear.

So, let us walk with heads held high,
In joyous praise, our voices nigh.
Through every challenge, we shall rise,
In love's embrace, we claim the skies.

Anointing of the Morning

In the hush of dawn's light, we pray,
Grace like whispers, gentle and bright.
Blessed hands anoint with heavenly care,
Softly draping the earth in prayer.

Morning dew clings to each blade,
A symphony of faith, never to fade.
Birds rise, their songs lift the soul,
In sacred communion, we feel whole.

Nature awakens beneath the sky,
Each heartbeat a hymn, a soft sigh.
The world in colors, fresh and pure,
In this moment, our hearts endure.

With each breath, the spirit sings,
In the embrace of love, joy springs.
Anointing our lives with hope anew,
In morning's glow, grace shines through.

We walk the path the light bestowed,
In the whispers of truth, we are shown.
Guided by faith, we journey forth,
In the anointing of morning, we find worth.

Wings of Redemption

Through shadows deep, the heart does soar,
On wings of mercy, we seek the shore.
In trials faced, the spirit's flight,
Brings forth the dawn from the darkest night.

Forgiveness blooms, a sacred art,
In brokenness, we find the start.
Each tear a seed, each wound a grace,
In the garden of love, we find our place.

With every step, redemption calls,
A whispering truth that never falls.
In the tapestry of light and dark,
Our souls are kindled, ignited spark.

Lifted high on faith's embrace,
We rise above, we find our space.
With hearts unveiled, we stand reborn,
In the wings of redemption, love is sworn.

Grace abounds in every stride,
In unity, the spirit guides.
Together we rise, united we thrive,
With wings of redemption, we come alive.

The Promise of the Dawn

In the silence, hope begins to stir,
A promise whispered, gently concur.
Each day unfolds a brand new grace,
In the dawn's embrace, we find our place.

The sun ascends, a golden sign,
A reminder that love's forever divine.
Through trials faced, we seek the light,
In the promise of dawn, faith takes flight.

New beginnings lie in every ray,
In the warmth of morning, fears decay.
With open hearts, we welcome the day,
The promise of dawn, our guiding way.

With whispered prayers, we lift our eyes,
To the heavens where our spirit flies.
In this sacred moment, we belong,
In the promise of the dawn, we are strong.

Together we stand, hand in hand,
In the beauty of life, we understand.
The dawn brings hope for every soul,
In love's embrace, we become whole.

Embrace of the Infinite

In the stillness, the infinite calls,
With arms outstretched, love never falls.
Each heartbeat echoes in divine grace,
In the embrace of the infinite, we find our place.

Stars whisper truths in the starry night,
Guiding our spirits with gentle light.
In the vastness, we are not alone,
In every prayer, the truth is sown.

The universe sings in a language pure,
In every moment, we must ensure.
The love we seek is always near,
In the embrace of the infinite, it is clear.

Waves of mercy wash over the shore,
In silence, we listen, we long for more.
With every breath, we journey deep,
In the embrace of love, we awaken from sleep.

Together we rise in a sacred dance,
In a world woven with divine chance.
The infinite waits as our hearts align,
In love's soft embrace, we intertwine.

Surrender to the Journey

In quiet whispers, call my name,
I walk the path, without a shame.
Faith's gentle hand, it leads me on,
Embracing light, until the dawn.

Through valleys deep and mountains high,
I feel the Spirit, always nigh.
With every step, I shed the weight,
Trusting the plan, I leave to fate.

The winds of change, they sing so sweet,
A melody that guides my feet.
In trial's fire, I find my grace,
A sacred bond, I now embrace.

The stars above, they twinkle bright,
Illuminating my search for light.
In surrender, I find my peace,
With every breath, my doubts release.

So on I go, with heart so free,
The journey's end is yet to be.
In humble trust, I take each chance,
In life's grand dance, I find my stance.

The Altar of Change

At the altar where shadows fade,
I offer hopes, unafraid.
In sacred silence, hearts align,
Transforming fear to love divine.

With open hands and willing soul,
I witness how the fragments whole.
From ashes rise, a spirit new,
In every trial, I learn what's true.

The seasons shift, a cycle spins,
In letting go, the journey begins.
Each moment holds a gift to share,
An invitation to love and care.

Through storms of doubt, I weather well,
In stormy seas, I find my shell.
Each wave that crashes teaches me,
To flow with grace, and simply be.

Upon this altar, I lay it all,
The fears I hold, the dreams that call.
With every sacrifice I yield,
I find my strength, my heart's true field.

Envisioning a New World

In visions bright, I see the light,
A world reborn, in love's pure sight.
Where hands unite in sacred grace,
Harmonious hearts, a warm embrace.

Each voice a note, in grand refrain,
Together singing through the pain.
With courage found, we rise as one,
Beneath the stars, we've just begun.

The wounds of old, they start to heal,
In every heart, compassion's seal.
With wisdom gained and spirits high,
We build a bridge to touch the sky.

Imagination paints the scene,
Of hope reborn, what could have been.
Together woven, threads of fate,
Creating futures, we co-create.

In every step, we pave the way,
For love's embrace to guide our stay.
With open hearts, we'll light the flame,
In envisioning, we find our name.

The Ascension of Joy

In joyous leap, I rise to fly,
With wings of hope, I touch the sky.
Each laugh a prayer, I send above,
In gratitude, I dance with love.

With every breath, the spirit sings,
Unlocking doors to hidden things.
In playful moments, grace unfolds,
In light and laughter, joy beholds.

The sunrise whispers sweetly near,
Inviting dreams, dispelling fear.
In the embrace of peace I stand,
A child of light, both free and grand.

In community, we share this bliss,
A sacred space, a gentle kiss.
Together rising, hand in hand,
We weave a tapestry so grand.

The ascension calls, a sacred rise,
In joyful hearts, the echoes lie.
With every beat, we celebrate,
In symphony, we elevate.

Guiding Stars of Tomorrow

In the night, they softly glow,
Guiding hearts where love can flow.
Each flicker speaks of dreams untold,
In their light, the future unfolds.

Whispers carried on the breeze,
Gentle echoes of holy pleas.
Faith ignites the darkest skies,
With every star, a chance to rise.

Holding hands, we walk the path,
Sharing joy, dispelling wrath.
Together we strive to find our way,
Underneath the skies of gray.

In the trials, hope prevails,
Through every storm, our spirit sails.
With guiding stars forever bright,
We journey forth towards the light.

Resurrection of the Spirit

From ashes roots a blossom fair,
Reviving life with tender care.
Through shadows deep, a voice resounds,
In silence, love's true heart is found.

The body fades, but souls take flight,
Awakening in endless light.
In every tear, a lesson lies,
Resurrecting hope that never dies.

With faith as wings, we soar above,
Uniting all with boundless love.
The spirit dances through the haze,
In sacred rhythms, we give praise.

Echoes of the past remain,
But future blooms from every pain.
In this cycle, we shall see,
Resurrection brings us free.

Melodies of the New Dawn

As dawn awakens, shadows flee,
Nature sings in harmony.
Each note a prayer, pure and bright,
Filling hearts with radiant light.

Sunrise paints the sky in gold,
Stories of the brave and bold.
Every chirp and breeze a tale,
In this symphony, we sail.

Unified, our voices rise,
A chorus praising endless skies.
In every heart, a sacred hymn,
A melody that won't grow dim.

With open arms, we greet the morn,
In its beauty, souls reborn.
Harmony embracing all,
In love's embrace, we shall not fall.

The Path to Enlightenment

Through winding trails, our spirits roam,
Seeking wisdom, finding home.
With each step on sacred ground,
In stillness, deeper truths are found.

The light within begins to shine,
Illuminating hearts divine.
Compassion guides our wayward feet,
In service, life becomes complete.

Beneath the stars, we ponder fate,
In unity, we resonate.
The questions asked through ages past,
In quietude, the answers last.

Transcending fears, we walk as one,
Embracing all — the moon, the sun.
On this path where spirits soar,
Enlightenment's forever more.

The Unveiling of Dreams

In silent prayer, the soul ignites,
A whispering hope in starry nights.
Guided by faith, we rise and soar,
Embracing visions, forevermore.

Through valleys deep, where shadows creep,
Promises of grace in the heart we keep.
With every tear, a seed is sown,
In fields of purpose, we are not alone.

The tapestry woven with threads so fine,
Each dream a promise, a sacred sign.
In the stillness, divine whispers call,
Inviting us to surrender it all.

As dawn breaks forth, the shadows flee,
Revealing paths to our destiny.
In the embrace of light, we find our way,
Awakening dreams that patiently lay.

With spirits unchained, we walk this land,
Together as one, united we stand.
In the unveiling of dreams, we see,
The beauty of life, in unity.

Shadows Give Way to Light

In the depths of night, where fears reside,
The flicker of hope, a gentle guide.
With every prayer, the heart takes flight,
As shadows give way to healing light.

Each tear that falls, a sacred stream,
Washing away the remnants of dream.
In the solace found, we rise anew,
For dawn's embrace brings a vibrant hue.

With open arms, we welcome grace,
Transforming sorrow in love's embrace.
Through trials faced, our spirits grow,
In the warmth of light, we come to know.

The path may twist, the road may bend,
But in unity, hearts shall mend.
For shadows linger, yet hope ignites,
As darkness yields to resplendent lights.

Together we stand, a radiant band,
With faith unbroken, hand in hand.
In the harmony of love's delight,
We blossom where shadows give way to light.

The Pilgrimage of Purpose

Upon the road where the faithful tread,
With heavy hearts and hopes widespread.
Each step a prayer, each breath a song,
In the pilgrimage of purpose, we belong.

Mountains rise high, rivers run clear,
Guiding the seekers, dispelling fear.
The journey unfolds in sacred grace,
Every challenge a chance to embrace.

With wisdom gleaned from trials faced,
Our spirits soar in the love embraced.
In the tapestry woven through pain and joy,
We find our calling, pure and coy.

In whispers of wind, the truth resounds,
The path of purpose in silence abounds.
Through valleys of doubt, the light will shine,
Illuminating the fate divine.

So let us walk with courage bold,
In the pilgrimage, our stories told.
Hand in hand, we stride with pride,
In purpose's name, we turn the tide.

Hearts Unbound

In the silence, where spirits connect,
Boundless love comes, we reflect.
Hearts unbound, rising like tides,
In the warmth of grace, the soul abides.

Through trials faced, we learn to rise,
With open hearts and watchful eyes.
In every kindness, a spark ignites,
Illumining paths, transcending nights.

Together we journey, hand in hand,
With faith as our guide, we take a stand.
In the dance of life, with joy we sway,
For hearts unbound shall light the way.

In the still moments, where love thrives,
A chorus echoes, our true lives.
Weaving the threads of compassion's embrace,
In unity found, we find our place.

So let our spirits forever roam,
In the symphony of love, we are home.
With hearts unbound, we sing, we play,
In timeless grace, we find our way.

Awakening Grace

In stillness waits the heart of man,
A whisper calls, a sacred plan.
The sun ascends with golden light,
Awakening grace, dispelling night.

In every breath, a chance to see,
The love that binds, the mystery.
With open arms, we rise anew,
Embracing hope, our spirits true.

The gentle breeze, a soothing balm,
In chaos found, a sacred calm.
With every step, we seek the face,
Of the divine in warm embrace.

Through trials faced, our faith will grow,
In darkest depths, His love will glow.
With eyes aflame, we lift our hands,
In gratitude, our spirit stands.

United hearts, we sing in praise,
In every moment, love conveys.
With every dawn, we find our place,
In depths of joy, awakening grace.

The Dawn of Promise

When shadows fall, there breaks a ray,
A promise made to guide our way.
In every moment, hope is sown,
The seeds of faith, in hearts are grown.

The morning light, a canvas bright,
Where dreams take flight, in pure delight.
A path unfolds, divinely paved,
In trust we stand, forever brave.

The world may tremble, storms may roar,
Yet in His hands, we find our shore.
With every breath, we claim His grace,
The dawn of promise, our sacred space.

In troubled times, we lift our song,
With love and faith, no fear is strong.
Each heartbeat echoes in the night,
The dawn will come, our guiding light.

Together rise, we stand as one,
In harmony, till day is done.
With every dawn, a chance we seize,
The promise lives, our hearts at ease.

From Ashes to Altars

From ashes cold, a fire ignites,
A spirit burns, with guiding lights.
What once was lost, reclaimed anew,
From ashes rise, the faithful few.

In trials faced, we find our voice,
In whispered prayers, we still rejoice.
The broken path, now beauty's way,
From ashes formed, to grace we pray.

Beyond the veil, the shadows fade,
In faith restored, our hope displayed.
With open hearts, we build the art,
From ashes bleak, to altars start.

The love we share, a sacred bond,
In every soul, a light responds.
From depths of sorrow, joy appears,
From ashes rise, releasing tears.

Together found, we lift our hands,
In unity, the promise stands.
From whispered dreams, to heights of praise,
From ashes made, to endless days.

Rebirth in Reverence

In silence deep, the heart beats slow,
A journey starts, where reverence flows.
With every leaf that falls in grace,
A rebirth blooms, the spirit's space.

In nature's hymn, we find the sound,
A sacred trust, forever bound.
With open arms, we welcome light,
In rebirth's glow, the soul takes flight.

The ancient paths of wisdom call,
In gentle whispers, hear them all.
In every shadow, lessons learned,
In sacred fires, our hearts are burned.

Together rise, we find our peace,
In every heartbeat, love's increase.
Through trials faced, our spirits find,
In rebirth's dance, our souls entwined.

With reverence deep, we stand as one,
In every moment, joy begun.
In sacred trust, forever free,
Rebirth in reverence, harmony.

Blooming in the Light

In gardens where the angels tread,
Petals unfold in prayerful cheer,
Awash with grace from heaven's bed,
Each bloom a whisper, soft and clear.

The sun bestows its golden glow,
Nurturing souls with love divine,
In every leaf, a tale they sow,
Of hope that flourishes in time.

With every dawn, new life appears,
As sacred breaths embrace the morn,
And in the stillness, joy draws near,
Where faith is nurtured, dreams are born.

The fragrance floats, a holy hymn,
A chorus rising from the earth,
Reminding us, through pain and whim,
Of boundless love, of endless worth.

We bloom in light, through shadows cast,
Emerging strong, like flowers bright,
With every trial that we've passed,
We find our path, we bloom in light.

Awash in Spirit

In the quiet, spirits rise,
A gentle flow, the heart's delight,
Awash in whispers, softest sighs,
In sacred moments, day and night.

The river of grace, it flows within,
Cleansing souls in sweet embrace,
Through every loss, and through each win,
We find our strength, our sacred space.

With faith as roots, and joy as leaves,
We stretch towards the heavens' call,
In every lesson, love believes,
Connecting all, uniting all.

Each tear a testament of love,
Each laugh a song of hope reborn,
Awash in spirit, we rise above,
In grace, we find the brightest morn.

Together, hearts lift in refrain,
With spirits soaring, hand in hand,
Awash in love, we break the chain,
To walk with grace across the land.

Sacred Moments of Renewal

In every dawn, a chance to start,
Moments whisper of rebirth,
A touch of grace upon the heart,
A song of hope fills barren earth.

The stillness speaks, in hushed tones,
As nature breathes, a sacred voice,
Each leaf that falls, each seed that sown,
Reminds us in our choice to rejoice.

A cycle turning, day by day,
In seasons' dance, the spirit grows,
Renewal comes, come what may,
In every storm, in every rose.

In tender moments, shadows flee,
As love embraces, pure and true,
Sacred bonds of unity,
Awakening the soul anew.

With every heartbeat, life returns,
In every prayer, a fire burns,
Sacred moments, wisdom earns,
In gentle waves, our spirit yearns.

Through the Veil of Time

Through the veil, a shimmer bright,
Where echoes of the past abide,
Each memory, a spark of light,
Guiding us on this sacred ride.

In timeless tales, we find our place,
The wise reflections of the ages,
Through trials faced, and paths we trace,
Our spirit grows, beyond the pages.

With every breath, we claim our role,
In the dance of life, both fierce and kind,
Through the veil of time, the soul,
Unraveling truths that we may find.

We walk in faith, our hearts ablaze,
With whispers of those gone before,
In every moment, we give praise,
For wisdom shared, for love's encore.

As stars align, our fates entwine,
Through the veil, we seek, we trust,
With spirits bold and hearts divine,
In the journey of life, we must.

Wings of Renewal

In the hush of dawn's embrace,
A whisper stirs the sleeping grace.
From shadows born, the light takes flight,
Renewing hearts with morning's light.

Old burdens shed like autumn leaves,
In cleansing rains, the spirit cleaves.
With faith anew, we rise and soar,
Wings of love, forevermore.

From trials faced, the soul's delight,
Emerges strong, a beacon bright.
Each tear has carved a path so true,
Leading us to skies so blue.

In every heart, a flame ignites,
Guided by celestial lights.
With courage found in every soul,
Together we make broken whole.

Oh, lift your eyes, see hope arise,
In every moment, the chance to rise.
For life is but a sacred dance,
In wings of renewal, we find our chance.

The Garden of Hope

Beneath the sky, where flowers bloom,
In tranquil soil, dispelling gloom.
A tender seed, once buried low,
Now reaches up, to breathe and grow.

Each petal bright, a prayer unfurls,
In gentle winds, a song of pearls.
The heart, a garden rich and fair,
With every root, a chance to care.

In silence, whispers weave their thread,
As dreams take shape, where angels tread.
With every raindrop, love descends,
In this haven, our spirit mends.

Through darkest nights, a glimmer shines,
In each hands' fold, a hope divine.
For every storm that brings us pain,
A brighter dawn will come again.

So nurture this, your sacred space,
With faith and trust, you'll find your place.
In the garden where hearts intertwine,
Abundant grace, forever shine.

From Ashes to Glory

In the embers of the night,
Hope emerges, burning bright.
From ashes cold, the fire's glow,
Awakens hearts to rise and flow.

Each fall has shaped the spirit strong,
In trials faced, we find the song.
With every loss, a lesson learned,
In depths of grief, compassion earned.

Through darkest paths, the soul will tread,
From broken clay, new forms are bred.
We rise again, with courage pure,
For in our scars, we are secure.

Like phoenix born from fiery fate,
In every struggle, we create,
A purpose found in pain's embrace,
From ashes rise, we claim our place.

So let us sing, our voices soar,
Together, united, we implore,
From ashes to the heights of glory,
A testament to our shared story.

The Path of Redemption

Upon this road, where shadows play,
We seek the light, a brand new day.
With weary hearts and footsteps slow,
We chart a course, our spirits grow.

Each stumble faced, a chance to mend,
Forgiveness blooms; we find a friend.
In every heart, the grace we share,
A journey divine, beyond despair.

For in the trials, we find our way,
The path of love will guide our stay.
With every choice, a step we take,
In faith's embrace, our fears will break.

Like rivers flow toward oceans deep,
Our souls unite, in love we leap.
No greater gift, than hearts made whole,
Redemption's song, the spirit's goal.

So walk with me, through night and day,
Embrace the light, come what may.
On this path, together we roam,
The path of redemption, our true home.

The Seraphim's Call

In skies of light, they softly sing,
With wings of fire, the praises ring.
Their voices lift to heavens high,
A sacred hymn, a pure reply.

Through realms untouched, their spirits guide,
In every heart, they shall abide.
With each embrace, they heal the pain,
In love's pure light, all truth shall reign.

These beings bright, in grace they dwell,
With every breath, they weave their spell.
A call to weary souls in night,
To seek the dawn, to find the light.

With gentle whispers, they impart,
A trust that stirs within the heart.
In every trial, their strength shall flow,
Through faith's embrace, we learn and grow.

So heed the call, ye humble souls,
For in their light, our spirit rolls.
Together bound, we rise and stand,
In seraph's grace, by fate's own hand.

The Tides of Transformations

In shadows deep, the waters churn,
With every wave, a lesson learned.
The tides of change, they ebb and flow,
In nature's dance, our spirits glow.

With every storm that shakes the shore,
A chance to rise, to seek for more.
The old must fade, the new shall claim,
And in this cycle, none is shamed.

The moon above, a guiding grace,
In her soft glow, we find our place.
With every phase, a truth revealed,
Our hearts unbound, our wounds are healed.

The journey long, with trials steep,
Yet in the depths, our faith runs deep.
With every swell, a soul reborn,
From ashes rise, the spirit worn.

So trust the tides, let go of fear,
For in the waves, the path is clear.
Though change may come, it's meant to be,
Embrace the flow, and you are free.

The Virtue of Hope

In the darkest hour, hope shall rise,
Like morning light in painted skies.
A beacon bright, it guides our way,
Through storms and trials, come what may.

With every breath, let faith ignite,
A flame within, dispelling night.
For every tear that falls in pain,
A promise waits for joy's refrain.

In silent whispers, dreams unfold,
Through trials faced, the heart grows bold.
With every step, a path is shown,
In hope's pure light, we're not alone.

The mountains high, we dare to climb,
With steady hearts, we mark our time.
For every struggle shapes our soul,
In hope's embrace, we are made whole.

So let us hold this virtue dear,
Through every shadow, every fear.
With hope as wings, we learn to soar,
A brighter world, forevermore.

In the Garden of Second Chances

In garden blooms, new life prevails,
Where every thorn, a tale entails.
With gentle hands, we tend the earth,
Each seed a dream, a precious birth.

The past may weigh, the heart may ache,
Yet in this space, our spirits wake.
A chance to grow, to heal the scars,
With every breath, we touch the stars.

The sun above, a golden glow,
Nurtures the seeds we choose to sow.
With patience taught by nature's grace,
We learn to rise, to find our place.

In every bud, a promise keeps,
A chance to thrive, the heart that leaps.
For life's a dance of loss and gain,
In second chances, love's refrain.

So walk with faith through every trial,
Embrace the journey, every mile.
In this garden, we find our way,
Together strong, come what may.

Divinity of Renewal

In the silence of dawn's light,
A whisper calls to the soul,
With each breath, a promise blooms,
Life's purpose, a sacred goal.

Through shadows of yesterday,
The spirit finds its way home,
Each tear sown, a seed of faith,
In grace, we're never alone.

The heart beats in sacred time,
Songs of love in the air,
A dance of divine mercy,
In unity, we prepare.

Mountains may rise in our path,
But courage fuels the rise,
Through storms we find our strength,
In trust, our spirit flies.

Embracing the cycle of change,
With each ending, a new start,
The spirit's flame, ever bright,
Awakens the hopeful heart.

Harmonies of Hope

In the stillness of the night,
Hope sings soft lullabies,
Melodies of timeless grace,
Whispering to the skies.

Every shadow holds a spark,
Every tear, a lesson learned,
In the depths of the struggle,
The flame of faith is burned.

Branches bend but do not break,
The roots dig deeper still,
With the wind beneath our wings,
We rise above the chill.

Hearts entwined in sacred bonds,
Together we share the weight,
Through the valleys we shall walk,
In love, we celebrate.

With every dawn, a new chance,
To embrace the gift of life,
Through the harmonies of hope,
We rise above the strife.

Seeds of the Spirit

In the garden of the soul,
Seeds of peace are gently sown,
With care and with intention,
In the heart, we've freely grown.

Each kindness offers a bloom,
Each love, a tender leaf,
In the warmth of shared moments,
We find our sweet relief.

With faith, we water the ground,
With hope, the sun will rise,
In the storms, we shelter each other,
Beneath the watchful skies.

Tales of grace and gentle strength,
Whispers in the wind arise,
As we cultivate our spirits,
In unity, we'll rise.

For the harvest is abundant,
When we share what's in our hearts,
Each soul a true reflection,
Of love that never departs.

Transcendence Through Trials

In the fire, we are forged,
Each challenge, a sacred test,
Through the struggles, we emerge,
More resilient and blessed.

The path may twist and turn,
Yet light breaks through the gloom,
Every trial teaches strength,
Every shadow leads to bloom.

As we rise from the ashes,
With hope lighting our way,
We find the keys to the future,
In love that guides each day.

With courage as our armor,
And faith a steady hand,
We build a bridge of promise,
To a future, bright and grand.

Transcendence is a journey,
In trials, we discover grace,
For every moment of struggle,
Is a chance for us to embrace.

Celestial Embrace

In whispers soft, the stars align,
A beckoning light, divine design.
Heaven's breath, on earth we feel,
In faith and love, our souls conceal.

With open hearts, we seek the way,
In silent prayer, we hope and say.
The moonlight guides us through the dark,
In every shadow, find the spark.

As spirits soar on wings of grace,
We find our home in warm embrace.
The universe, a sacred scroll,
In every part, we find our whole.

A dance of light upon the sea,
The waves of hope, they set us free.
In every heartbeat, truth unfolds,
In every story, love retolds.

In unity, our voices rise,
A symphony that fills the skies.
With every breath, we praise the day,
In harmony, we walk the way.

The Seed of Tomorrow

In gentle soil, a promise lies,
A seed of hope 'neath azure skies.
With light and love, it starts to grow,
The path of grace, we come to know.

Each droplet falls, a tender kiss,
As roots reach deep, we find our bliss.
The sunbeams warm, the branches sway,
In sacred whispers, we shall stay.

The world awaits, a harvest bright,
In every heart, the will to light.
With faith as guide and dreams in hand,
We nurture life upon this land.

Through trials faced, our strength will rise,
In every tear, a spirit cries.
Yet from the dark, our courage blooms,
In every ending, life resumes.

Together, we will sow the seeds,
In every heart, compassion bleeds.
With every choice, we pave the way,
To brighter tomorrows, come what may.

Heavens Open Wide

Lift up your gaze to skies so bright,
The heavens open, spilling light.
In every star, a story told,
Of love eternal, brave and bold.

The angels sing in sweet refrain,
A melody to ease our pain.
In every note, a soul set free,
Awakening our harmony.

With every dawn, a chance renewed,
In every heart, the joy imbued.
The grace that flows, a river wide,
In faith and hope, we shall abide.

As clouds disperse, the sun will rise,
A glorious dance in azure skies.
With lifted voices, we proclaim,
The love that binds, in holy name.

In unity, we find our strength,
As we embrace the cosmic length.
Together, we shall pave the way,
For rising hope, a brand new day.

The Sacred Rebirth

From ashes born, the phoenix flies,
In death, we find new hope that lies.
In every end, a start we claim,
The sacred cycle, life's true aim.

In shadows cast, the light will gleam,
A promised dawn, a vibrant dream.
With every breath, we shall renew,
In faith and love, we'll see it through.

The whispers of the past still call,
Yet in the now, we stand up tall.
With every scar, a story shines,
In every challenge, strength defines.

The winter's chill gives way to spring,
In every heart, a song to sing.
The sacred dance of time unfolds,
In every moment, life beholds.

Together, hand in hand we rise,
With open hearts and hopeful eyes.
In unity, we break the chains,
Through sacred rebirth, love remains.

A Canvas of New Horizons

In the embrace of dawn's soft light,
We see the canvas, pure and bright.
With hope as our guiding brush,
We paint the dreams without a rush.

Each color sings of faith and grace,
Reflecting the Creator's face.
New horizons beckon boldly near,
In every heart, His whispers clear.

With every stroke, a promise made,
In the quiet, our fears allayed.
Together, we create, we share,
A masterpiece beyond compare.

Let love be the palette we choose,
Each hue a chance we will not lose.
In unity, we craft our way,
Towards the dawn of a brighter day.

As shadows fade and light appears,
We tread on paths devoid of fears.
A canvas stretched across the skies,
Reflecting truth that never dies.

The Rebirth of Innocence

In the stillness of the sacred night,
The stars awaken, pure and bright.
Whispers of old bring forth the new,
In every heart, a promise true.

Like blossoms springing after rain,
Innocence breaks free from pain.
A child's laughter fills the air,
Reminding us of love laid bare.

With every dawn, grace we reclaim,
In simplicity, we find His name.
A gentle touch, a soft embrace,
In each moment, we find His grace.

As shadows flee and light expands,
United, we join our hands.
The rebirth swells in hearts that seek,
In every soul, His joy unique.

To cherish dreams, to hold them dear,
To live anew, to cast out fear.
Through every trial, we shall rise,
In innocent faith, we touch the skies.

Forging the Future

In the furnace of love, our spirits blend,
Together we rise, our hearts ascend.
With every challenge that we face,
We find the strength of our sacred place.

The hammer falls, the sparks ignite,
In unity, we embrace the light.
Forged in trials, tempered by strife,
Each moment we shape a new life.

With visions of hope, we carve the path,
In the balance of love, we quell the wrath.
A tapestry woven with threads of grace,
In every heartbeat, His heart we trace.

The echoes of faith guide us still,
Each dream a spark, each act our will.
Together we stand, no fear to greet,
Forging the future at destiny's feet.

As the dawn breaks, our spirits soar,
In the forge of creation, we yearn for more.
In hope and love, our purpose shines,
Creating a world where peace entwines.

The Ripple of Grace

In the still pond where silence reigns,
A single drop, the echo gains.
Rippling outward, spreading wide,
A touch of grace we cannot hide.

The gentle flow, a loving stream,
In every heart, a sacred dream.
With kindness cast like seeds in soil,
Compassion blooms, our souls embroil.

Each act of love, a wave we send,
A cycle of grace that has no end.
In unity, a chorus sings,
Of hope and joy, such beauty brings.

The ripple touch, it grows and swells,
In every prayer, His presence dwells.
Through laughter shared and burdens eased,
A legacy of love is seized.

As echoes fade, new waves arise,
In every heart, His promise lies.
Through grace we walk, with spirits high,
On the canvas of life, together we fly.

Prayers for the New Path

With each step anew, we journey forth,
Guided by faith, revealed in the north.
Hands clasped in unity, hearts open wide,
We walk hand in hand, with God as our guide.

Each dawn brings a promise, a chance to renew,
Whispers of hope in the morning dew.
In the silence we gather, our spirits arise,
Finding the strength in each other's eyes.

Beneath the vast heavens, our voices unite,
Praising the journey that leads us to light.
Through valleys of shadow, we shall not fear,
For love is the compass that brings us near.

In moments of doubt, we raise up our song,
For faith is a melody, steadfast and strong.
With prayers like petals, we scatter our pleas,
A garden of hope that dances in the breeze.

Together in spirit, we forge our own fate,
For tomorrow awaits, it is never too late.
May the grace that surrounds us guide our true path,
In prayers we awaken, in joy we shall laugh.

The Dawn Chorus

In the hush of the morning, a song starts to play,
Voices of angels at the break of the day.
Each note a reminder, of blessings we share,
A chorus of whispers that fill the cool air.

The sun peeks through clouds, soft light on the face,
Nature rejoicing in sacred embrace.
With hearts full of wonder, we rise from our sleep,
Finding the treasures that morning will keep.

Birds glide through branches, a dance in the sky,
A tapestry woven from earth's lullaby.
We join in the harmony, spirits set free,
Attuned to the rhythm of life's melody.

Embracing the stillness, we breathe in the light,
Filled with the promise of love burning bright.
In every soft whisper, a prayer takes its flight,
In the dawn chorus, our souls find delight.

From shadows to sunrise, in moments we rise,
Together we gather, with hope in our eyes.
So let the dawn speak, let our spirits soar,
In the heart of the morning, we're destined for more.

A Covenant with Tomorrow

We stand at the threshold, with trust in our hearts,
Binding our futures, as each new day starts.
With promises whispered, we vow to believe,
In the beauty of life, and the love we receive.

Should shadows encircle, we'll walk through the night,
For hope is our lantern, it guides us with light.
In storms we'll find shelter, our faith will not bend,
For the strength of our bond will never know end.

Each moment a canvas, with colors of grace,
In the tapestry woven, we find our true place.
No fear of tomorrow, nor doubt that can stay,
For together we conquer, in love's endless way.

In laughter and sorrow, we'll cherish the grind,
By nurturing kindness, our hearts intertwined.
Through trials and triumphs, our spirits align,
A covenant sacred, forever divine.

So let us embrace what the future will bring,
With joy as our anthem, our souls will take wing.
In unity forward, we live and we grow,
A promise to cherish, in each ebb and flow.

The Radiance of Possibility

In the stillness of night, dreams flicker and glow,
Casting glimpses of light where hope dares to go.
We gather the stars, each wish like a seed,
Planted in faith, where our spirits are freed.

With eyes set on horizons, we strive to attain,
The beauty in hardship, the joy in the pain.
Like rivers we flow, we bend and we twist,
Carving our path in a world often missed.

In every new moment, potential ignites,
Awakening courage, ascending new heights.
With hearts wide open, we breathe in the air,
Finding the purpose that whispers our prayer.

In the tapestry woven, each thread holds a story,
In shadows and light, we discover our glory.
Together, resilient, we rise from the fall,
Embracing the journey, we answer the call.

So let us shine brightly, like candles at dusk,
For the radiance living in hope is a must.
In the choir of life, let our voices resound,
In the embrace of tomorrow, true beauty is found.

A Covenant of Fresh Starts

In the light of grace, we gather near,
With hearts open wide, casting out fear.
Every dawn whispers of hope anew,
A promise of peace in all that we do.

We walk hand in hand on this sacred path,
Embracing the lessons to withstand the wrath.
Through trials and storms, our spirits align,
In covenant bound, our souls intertwine.

Renewed in spirit, we rise and rejoice,
In unity found, we strengthen our voice.
With faith as our guide, each step is divine,
A tapestry woven, through love we divine.

Let light shine forth, dispelling the night,
In every corner, we seek His great light.
For in every heart, a flame does burn bright,
A covenant forged in love's purest sight.

So take up the call, embrace the new day,
Together in faith, we'll find our own way.
The journey ahead, with trust, we will chart,
In every fresh start, a beating of heart.

The Transformative Journey

In the silence of dawn, we hear His call,
A whisper of change, a promise to all.
Through valleys of shadows, our spirits will climb,
Awakening souls, transcending through time.

Each step we take, another is paved,
In search for the light, the lost will be saved.
With each breath we take, a chance to be whole,
The transformative journey ignites every soul.

Through rivers of doubt, we'll wade without fear,
His presence beside us, ever so near.
Each struggle we face, a lesson bestowed,
In faith and in love, our path will unfold.

The mountains may rise, the winds may howl,
Yet courage within us, we still will prowl.
For strength comes like rivers, from hearts that believe,
In every new chapter, we learn to conceive.

Bearing witness to change, we honor the grace,
In the depth of our trials, His light we embrace.
United we stand, our purpose declared,
Through faith's endless journey, our spirits ensnared.

So traverse with intent, in love's sacred name,
In the journey of life, never fear the flame.
For shadows may linger, but joy breaks the dawn,
In the transformative path, we forever move on.

Illuminated Souls

In the still of the night, the stars brightly shine,
Illuminated souls, as if by design.
Each glimmer a blessing, a promise of grace,
Reflecting our journey, each moment we trace.

With hearts stitched in faith, we gather as one,
Embracing the trials, our battle's begun.
In kindness and mercy, our spirits unite,
To navigate darkness and seek out the light.

From ashes of doubt, new visions arise,
Hope springs eternal beneath the vast skies.
Through prayers we ascend, transcending the pain,
In illuminated souls, love's power remains.

As echoes of wisdom resonate deep,
In this sacred dance, our burdens we keep.
For every lost tear, a new joy we find,
Our hearts intertwined, united and kind.

So let our light shine, unyielding and bright,
In the darkest of places, we'll be the first light.
For in every spirit, a promise unfolds,
As we walk together, our stories retold.

With each passing moment, we cherish His grace,
In illuminated souls, we find our place.
Together we rise, unbroken and whole,
In love everlasting, we flourish, we roll.

The Song of Renewal

In the hush of the morn, a melody starts,
The song of renewal sings deep in our hearts.
With every soft note, the past fades away,
Emerging in beauty, we greet the new day.

With voices united, we rise and we sing,
As joy spreads its wings, our praises take wing.
In harmony woven, our spirits take flight,
In love's sweet embrace, we bask in the light.

The rhythms of grace dance through ancient trees,
A testament spoken by whispers of breeze.
Each leaf tells a story, of change and rebirth,
In the song of renewal, we celebrate earth.

Through valleys of sorrow, through mountains of grace,
We find strength in unity, love's sweet embrace.
In trials and triumphs, our voices will call,
In the song of our souls, His blessings for all.

So let the notes linger, let joy be our guide,
In each heartfelt chorus, let love abide.
For life is a symphony we all can compose,
In the song of renewal, our true spirit grows.

With every new dawn, let our voices resound,
In the song of renewal, our souls will be found.
Together we stand, as one we shall sing,
In the sacred embrace of love's precious ring.

Milton Keynes UK
Ingram Content Group UK Ltd.
UKHW021835301124
451618UK00007BA/155

9 789916 897782